MAXIMUM SPEED

MAGNIFICENT
MOTORCYCLES

ROB COLSON

Enslow
PUBLISHING

Published in 2023 by Enslow Publishing, LLC
29 East 21st Street, New York, NY 10010

Series editor: John Hort
Designer: Ben Ruocco
Produced by Tall Tree Ltd

Manufactured in the United States of America

CPSIA compliance information: Batch #CSENS23: For further information contact
Enslow Publishing LLC, New York, New York at 1-800-398-2504.

Please visit our website, www.enslowpublishing.com. For a free color catalog of all our high-quality books,
call toll free 1-800-398-2504 or fax 1-877-980-4454.

Cataloging-in-Publication Data

Names: Colson, Rob.
Title: Magnificent motorcycles / Rob Colson.
Description: New York : Enslow Publishing, 2023. | Series: Maximum speed | Includes glossary and index.
Identifiers: ISBN 9781978531062 (pbk.) | ISBN 9781978531086 (library bound) | ISBN 9781978531079 (6pack) | ISBN
   9781978531093 (ebook)
Subjects: LCSH: Motorcycles--Juvenile literature.
Classification: LCC TL440.15 C66 2023 | DDC 629.227'5--dc23 Names: Colson, Rob.

Find us on

CONTENTS

POWER ON TWO
WHEELS

The first practical bicycles were developed in the 1860s. Soon afterwards, engineers and inventors started experimenting to find ways to power bicycles with engines. By the end of the nineteenth century, motorcycles powered by gas engines were being made around the world.

▼ STEAM MOTORCYCLES

The first motorcycles were powered by steam. Two versions were made in the late 1860s. French engineer Louis-Guillaume Perreaux (1806–1889) and American inventor Sylvester Roper (1823–1896) both appear to have had the idea to attach a small steam engine to a bicycle frame around the same time. Roper died while testing his motorcycle (below). During his final ride, he was timed at a top speed of 39 miles (64 km) per hour.

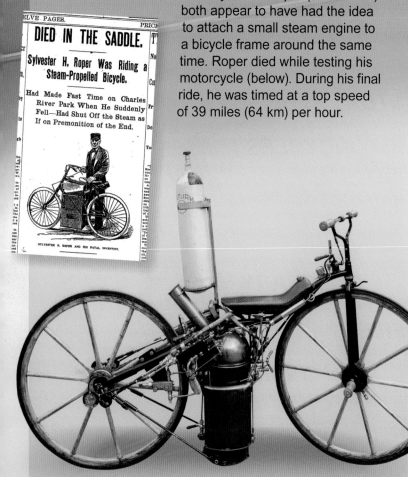

DIED IN THE SADDLE.

Sylvester H. Roper Was Riding a Steam-Propelled Bicycle.

Had Made Fast Time on Charles River Park When He Suddenly Fell—Had Shut Off the Steam as If on Premonition of the End.

SYLVESTER H. ROPER AND HIS FATAL INVENTION.

EARLY SPEED

1867–69
Roper Steam Velocipede, USA
Top speed | 40 miles (64 km) per hour

FIRST GAS ENGINE

The first motorcycle powered by a **gas engine** was the Reitwagen, made by German inventors Gottlieb Daimler (1834–1900) and Wilhelm Maybach (1846–1929). The Reitwagen was hot, noisy, unreliable, and slow, with a top speed of 6.8 miles (11 km) per hour. However, the idea of a motorcycle powered by a gas engine quickly caught on, and the first **production motorcycle**, by German manufacturer Hildebrand & Wolfmüller, went on sale in 1894.

Gottlieb Daimler

Wilhelm Maybach

Hildebrand & Wolfmüller production motorcycle

The Reitwagen

RACING MOTORCYCLES

As soon as motorcycles became widely available, people started to race them. The first organized race was held in England in 1897, and shortly afterwards races were being held around the world as the motorcycles became faster and more exciting to ride. Within a few years, motorcycles were being made by companies across Europe and the United States. Motorcycles became more reliable, reaching top speeds in excess of 43 miles (70 km) per hour.

1885
Reitwagen, Germany
Top speed | 6.8 miles (11 km) per hour

1894
Hildebrand & Wolfmüller, Germany
Top speed | 28 miles (45 km) per hour

1905
Triumph Model 3HP, England
Top speed | 40 miles (64 km) per hour

SPEED
RECORDS

The first motorcycle speed record was set in 1903, when American Glenn Curtiss was clocked at 64 miles (103 km) per hour. Since 1920, records have been certified by the International Federation of Motorcycling (FIM). The rider must complete two runs of the same course in opposite directions.

 SETTING THE PACE

In 1911, Glenn Curtiss (1878–1930) set the land speed record for any vehicle on a motorcycle that he had built himself, reaching a top speed of 136 miles (219 km) per hour. This is the only time the land speed record has been held by a motorcycle.

MOTORCYCLE SPEED RECORD

1907
Curtiss V8 | 136 miles (219 km) per hour
Ridden by American Glenn Curtiss

1937
BMW 500cc | 174 miles (279.5 km) per hour
Ridden by German Ernst Jakob Henne

1956
NSU Delphin III | 210 miles (339 km) per hour
Ridden by Wilhelm Hertz

⌄ ADDING FAIRINGS

Between 1929 and 1937, German Ernst Jakob Henne (1904–2005) broke the world speed record seven times riding BMW motorcycles. His 1937 record stood for 14 years. To maximize his speed, Henne rode motorcycles that were fitted with full **fairings**. These formed a smooth metal shell that covered the frame of the motorcycle, reducing the force of **drag**, which slows the motorcycle down.

——— *Ernst Jakob Henne wore a special aerodynamic helmet.*

⌄ STREAMLINERS

In the 1950s, riders set new records riding a new kind of motorcycle that was built for speed. The rider sat encased inside an aerodynamic shell to minimize drag. These motorcycles were known as streamliners. German rider Wilhelm Hertz (1912–1998) set three new records on his NSU Delphin streamliners, riding on the flat course at the Bonneville Salt Flats in Utah.

1970
Yamaha 'Big Red' | 251 miles (405 km) per hour
Ridden by American Don Vesco

2010
Ack Attack | 376 miles (606 km) per hour
Ridden by American Rocky Robinson

1980
Easyriders streamliner | 322 miles (518 km) per hour
Ridden by American Dave Campos

GRAND PRIX
RACING

Motorcycle Grand Prix races are held on circuits around roads or purpose-built tracks. The riders use racing motorcycles designed for speed and agility. There are four different divisions of Grand Prix racing, with three for gas engines and one for electric motorcycles. The fastest division is called MotoGP.

⌄ RACING SEASON

In a Grand Prix season, a series of 20 races are held across the world. The races vary in length between 59 miles (95 km) and 80 miles (130 km), and are over in around 40 minutes. On race day, Moto3 is run first, followed by Moto2. The top division, MotoGP, races last. Young riders usually start in Moto3. If they are successful, they can move up to the faster divisions.

The highest speed in a MotoGP race was set by Italian Andrea Dovizioso, riding a Ducati. He was clocked at 221 miles (356 km) per hour at the 2018 Italian Grand Prix.

⌃ STAR RIDER

Italian Valentino Rossi (born 1979) is one of the most successful MotoGP riders ever. Between 2001 and 2009, he won the MotoGP World Championship seven times. In 2005, Rossi invented a new maneuver when he stuck out his leg to keep his balance when taking a corner. Known as the "leg dangle," it soon caught on, and now most riders do it.

🔥 RACING MOTORCYCLES

MotoE
Electric motor
Top speed | 167 miles (270 km) per hour

MotoGP
Engine size | 1,000 cc
Top speed | 224 miles (361 km) per hour

Moto3
Engine size | 250 cc
Top speed 154 miles (248 km) per hour

Moto2
Engine size | 765 cc
Top speed | 187 miles (301 km) per hour

⌄ EXTREME LEAN

Motorcycle riders wear pads on their knees to protect them when they take turns. This is because motorcycles turn by leaning into the direction of the curve. MotoGP riders hang off the side of their motorcycles when they take corners and lean at an angle of up to 64 degrees from vertical. At this angle, only a patch of the tires the size of a credit card is in contact with the track. The tires are made from a special rubber to produce enough **grip** from this tiny patch to avoid sliding.

‹ MOTOE

In 2019, a new Grand Prix series called MotoE was started for motorcycles powered by electric motors. All riders use the same Energica Ego Corsa motorcycle, making it a pure test of riding skill. The races are short and sharp, over less than 18 miles (30 km) total distance. The first season was won by Italian rider Matteo Ferrari (born 1997).

ISLE OF MAN
TT RACE

The Isle of Man TT is one of the oldest and most prestigious motorcycle races in the world. First held in 1907, the week-long event consists of a series of time trials. Riders race against the clock around public roads on the Isle of Man, a small island in the Irish Sea.

⌄ DEMANDING CIRCUIT

The main races are held on the Snaefell Mountain Course. This long circuit is a test of riding skill. It is 37.7 miles (60.7 km) long, with more than 200 bends along often bumpy public roads. Riders climb from sea level to an **altitude** of 1,312 feet (400 m) and speed back down again.

Isle of Man

Sulby Straight is the fastest point on the course, where New Zealand rider Bruce Anstey was clocked at a record 206 miles (332 km) per hour during practice in 2006.

Ballaugh Bridge is where riders jump into the air as they cross a humpbacked bridge.

Hailwood Rise is the climb to the highest point on the course.

Union Mills is a fast section that is popular with spectators.

Start/finish line

TT LEGEND

Northern Irish rider Joey Dunlop (1952–2000) was the most successful rider ever at the Isle of Man TT, winning a record 26 races, including hat tricks of three wins in one year in 1985, 1988, and 2000. Tragically, he died a few weeks after his last Isle of Man TT in a race in Tallinn, Estonia, where he lost control of his motorcycle in wet conditions.

EXTREME DANGER

The Isle of Man TT has been described as the most dangerous race in the world. Between 1907 and 2019, 151 riders died during official races or practice sessions. Along many sections of the course, the tight public roads are lined with trees, buildings or stone walls. With riders regularly reaching speeds of up to 199 miles (320 km) per hour along the straight sections, the tiniest of mistakes can be fatal.

Lap record:
16 minutes 43 seconds

set by Peter Hickman in 2019 on a BMW S1000RR.
That's an average speed of

135 miles per hour

ENDURANCE
RACING

For some riders, the ultimate test of riding ability is provided by endurance events. In races that can last for days or even weeks, riders must maintain their concentration as they keep their speeds up for hour after hour, often riding over extreme terrain.

＞ DAKAR RALLY

The Dakar Rally is an endurance event in which vehicles race across deserts, crossing rough off-road terrain. The race was first held in 1977, starting in Paris, France, and finishing in Dakar, Senegal. Competitors covered a distance of 6,214 miles (10,000 km) and crossed the Sahara Desert. The race has also been held in South America, and in 2020, it was held in the Arabian Desert in Saudi Arabia for the first time. There are separate categories for cars, trucks, motorcycles, and quad motorcycles, which are motorcycles with four wheels (above). Competitors complete set **stages** each day of the rally.

⌄ ENDURANCE WORLD CHAMPIONSHIP

The Endurance World Championship is a series of five endurance races with a duration of between 8 and 24 hours. Teams of two or three riders take turns on the same motorcycle. The most grueling race of all is the 24-hour Motos race held on the Bugatti Circuit at Le Mans, France. The teams complete a distance of more than 2,175 miles (3,500 km) at an average speed of 93 miles (150 km) per hour.

⌃ ULTIMATE TEST

The toughest riders in the Dakar Rally compete in a special category called the Original by Motul. In this category, the riders must complete the rally without any outside assistance. If their motorcycle breaks down, the riders have to fix it themselves. Each competitor is allowed one piece of luggage for their personal belongings, which is carried for them by a support truck. The support truck also carries a large tool kit for riders to use to repair their motorcycles in the camp at the end of each stage.

‹ RIDE AROUND THE WORLD

In October 1912, American Carl Stearns Clancy (1890–1971) set sail from New York at the start of an epic adventure around the world. Riding a Henderson Four motorcycle, Clancy completed his journey in August 1913. He had ridden a total of 18,020 miles (29,000 km) across Europe, Africa, Asia, and North America to become the first person to ride a motorcycle right around the world.

MOTORCYCLES

*The fastest motorcycles in the world cannot be taken on the roads. To qualify as road-legal, **high-performance** motorcycles are often fitted with speed-limiters. However, in 2015 Japanese manufacturer Kawasaki released a new model that could be taken past these limits to become the fastest motorcycle on the road.*

To minimize drag, Rollie Free wore just a pair of swimming trunks and lay flat on the motorcycle with his legs stretched behind him.

⌃ BLACK LIGHTNING

Manufactured between 1948 and 1952, the Vincent Black Lightning was the fastest production motorcycle in the world for 35 years. In 1948, American rider Rollie Free (1900–1984) rode it to a speed of 150 miles (242 km) per hour at the Bonneville Salt Flats. In 1951, a **supercharged** edition of the Black Lightning was taken to a then-world-record about 60 miles (290 km) per hour. Only 31 models were ever made. One was sold in 2018 for $929,000, making it the most expensive motorcycle in history.

⌄ NINJA H2

The Kawasaki Ninja H2 has been the fastest street-legal motorcycle in the world since 2015, with a top speed of 209 miles (337 km) per hour. Its extra power comes from a specially designed supercharger. This was Kawasaki's first supercharged production motorcycle in more than 30 years. The H2R is a modified Ninja created specially for racing. With lightweight, carbon fiber body parts and a special titanium **exhaust**, the H2R has a top speed of 248 miles (400 km) per hour.

SUPERCHARGED

A supercharger is a device that forces extra air into an engine. This allows the fuel to burn more quickly, increasing the engine's power. Kawasaki first added a supercharger to a road motorcycle in 1978. This increased power by nearly 50 percent, but it made the motorcycle hard to handle. Superchargers fell out of favor until Kawasaki came up with a new, improved version for the Ninja H2 engine (above).

CRUISING
MOTORCYCLES

Cruising motorcycles are built for power and comfort rather than extreme speed. These heavy motorcycles have engines that are as big as the engines in a family car. Powerful and often very noisy, they are the perfect motorcycles for members of motorcycle clubs who like to take to the roads together on the weekend.

❯ HONDA GOLD WING

Japanese manufacturer Honda has made the luxury Gold Wing model since 1974. The 2018 model is the Gold Wing 2018 GL1800. It has a six-**cylinder**, 1.8-liter engine. The motorcycle is fitted with a computer-controlled electronic **transmission**. Sensors monitor the road conditions and adjust the transmission for the best possible performance, depending on whether they detect a smooth highway or a bumpy mountain road.

The angle of the Gold Wing's windscreen can be changed at the push of a button.

HARLEY DAVIDSON CVO

Harley Davidson is world-renowned for its stylish motorcycles. The CVO is a range of the biggest, most luxurious motorcycles Harley Davidson have ever made. The limited-edition machines are fitted with huge 1.9-liter Milwaukee-Eight 117 engines. The two cylinders are arranged in a "V" shape. They are fitted with four **valves** to regulate the fuel and air flow, rather than the usual two. This gives the engine 10 percent more power.

*Captain America is a chopper that appeared in the 1969 movie Easy Rider. It is a Harley Davidson with extra-long front **forks**.*

CHOPPERS

The chopper is a style of customized motorcycle that was first made in California in the 1950s. These are big cruisers that have been radically altered by their owners, who have fitted them with long forks at the front to give them a stretched-out look. The rider can typically sit upright on the motorcycle with a straight back.

MOTORCYCLE CLUBS

The first motorcycle clubs were formed in the early twentieth century to allow riders to come together and exchange information. In the 1950s, a new kind of "outlaw" club started to form in the United States. The club members rode large cruisers that were often extremely customized, and wore patches on their riding leathers to show which club they belonged to. The most famous outlaw club is the Hells Angels, whose members normally ride Harley Davidsons.

DIRT
BIKING

Racing over rough terrain, motocross riders ride specially made off-road dirt bikes. These are light motorcycles made to withstand the bumps and jumps of rough terrain. Motocross is a relatively affordable form of racing, and amateur riders often meet up for races at temporary tracks built around a field.

> WHAT MAKES A DIRT BIKE?

Dirt bikes are lightweight, made with many plastic parts rather than heavier metal. The knobby tires provide plenty of grip in the dirt. The motorcycles are fitted with a long suspension, which means that the wheels are very flexible. This allows riders to take jumps at high speed and land safely.

∧ KTM 450 SX-F

The KTM 450 SX-F is the fastest dirt bike in the world, with a top speed in a straight line of 123 miles (198 km) per hour. However, dirt bikes are not built primarily for speed, and during a race around a tight course, the riders are usually going under 37 miles (60 km) per hour. The thrills come from the hills and jumps rather than the speed.

MOTOCROSS WORLD CHAMPIONSHIP

In motocross races, riders compete around tight dirt tracks with plenty of humps, bumps, and jumps along the way. The top motocross competition is the Motocross World Championship for 450 cc motorcycles, which is held over 19 rounds in venues across Europe, Asia, and South America. Riders compete in two hectic half-hour races at each venue.

In sidecar motocross races, a sidecar is attached to the bike. As the dirt bikes cannot lean into corners, the passenger must continuously shift their weight from side to side.

DIRT BIKE LEGEND

Italian rider Antonio Cairoli (born 1985) has been crowned Motocross World Champion a record nine times. He was well on his way towards a tenth title in 2019 after winning seven of the first 10 races, but he missed the rest of the season after dislocating his shoulder. Cairoli's riding style is aggressive but smooth, and he is at his very best in tough sandy conditions when others often struggle.

SPEEDWAY
RACING

Speedway is a form of motorcycle racing on an oval dirt track. Races are fast and furious as four riders battle around four laps of the track. Speedway bikes reach maximum speeds of around 68 miles (110 km) per hour along the straight sections of the track.

FIRST SPEEDWAY

Speedway racing first started in Australia in the 1920s, and soon spread to Europe and North America. By the 1930s, speedway was attracting huge crowds of up to 50,000 spectators. The sport's popularity has since declined, but speedway still has a loyal following in many European countries.

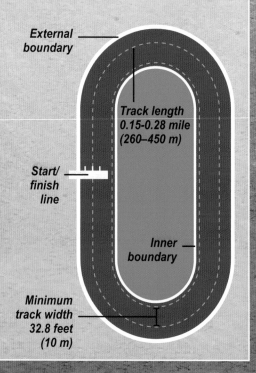

External boundary

Track length 0.15-0.28 mile (260–450 m)

Start/ finish line

Inner boundary

Minimum track width 32.8 feet (10 m)

⌃ BOARD TRACK RACING

In the 1910s and 1920s in the United States, races were held on wooden tracks. The tilted corners allowed the riders to take them at high speeds. One track in New Jersey had corners banked at 45 degrees, and riders could complete a lap of the 0.12 mile (200 m) track in less than eight seconds. Accidents were common and many riders were killed.

BROADSIDING

Speedway bikes have just one gear and no brakes. This means that riders need to use a special technique called broadsiding to take corners. They slide the rear wheel towards the outside of the bend, while the front wheel continues to point to the front. This is where races are often won or lost, as the most skillful riders lose the least speed as they broadside.

ICE SPEEDWAY

In Russia and Scandinavia, a special form of winter speedway has been developed. The rules are similar to those for dirt tracks, but the track is made of ice. The tires are fitted with metal spikes (below, left) to help them to grip the slippery track. This means that riders cannot broadside around corners. Instead, they lean their bikes into the corner so that the handlebars nearly touch the track!.

STUNT
RIDERS

Stunt riders perform a range of death-defying tricks on motorcycles. Some riders specialize in tricks such as wheelies, while others launch themselves high into the air from ramps.

RAMP-TO-RAMP

The most spectacular and dangerous motorcycle stunt of all is the ramp-to-ramp jump, in which a rider flies through the air. The rider accelerates towards the launch ramp to achieve maximum speed at the point of takeoff. Once in the air, they must control the motorcycle and angle the wheels down so that they can land safely on the ramp at the end of the jump. The world-record distance in a ramp-to-ramp jump is held by Australian Robbie Maddison (born 1981), who covered a distance of 351 feet (107 m) in 2008. That's almost as long as a football field!

DAREDEVIL PERFORMER

American Hazel Eaton (1895–1970) rode the Wall of Death at circuses around the United States in the 1920s. She would wow audiences by riding her motorcycle at speeds of up to 62 miles (100 km) per hour, often with her hands away from the handlebars. During one performance, she narrowly escaped death when the brakes on her motorcycle locked, causing her to suddenly lose speed and crash to the ground. After several weeks in hospital, the fearless Eaton climbed right back on her motorcycle and rode the wall.

WALL OF DEATH

The motordrome, or Wall of Death, is a stunt in which motorcycles ride around the near-vertical sides of a circular track. The riders seemingly defy gravity by maintaining a speed of at least 31 miles (50 km) per hour. At this speed, the wall pushes back against the rider with enough force to counter the force of gravity that pulls them down.

EVEL KNIEVEL

American Evel Knievel (1938–2007) made more than 200 ramp-to-ramp jumps. He survived 15 crashes, during which he broke more than 40 different bones. Knievel's most spectacular crash came in 1974, when he attempted to cross the Snake River Canyon in Idaho, in a rocket-powered motorcycle called the Skycycle X-2. His parachute opened too early and he fell to the bottom of the canyon. Knievel had hoped to achieve speeds of over 372 miles (600 km) per hour in his rocket motorcycle.

FASTEST WHEELIE

The Motorcycle Wheelie World Championship is held each year in Yorkshire, England. Riders compete with one another to perform the fastest wheelie (riding with just the rear wheel on the ground). In 2017, Irish rider Ted Brady (born 1970) set the world record for the fastest-ever wheelie by completing a 0.62 mile (1 km) course on one wheel at an average speed of 218 miles (351 km) per hour.

DRAG MOTORCYCLES

Drag motorcycles race one another on a straight 0.24 mile (400 m track). Blink and you'll miss it, as these explosive races are over in seconds. The biggest drag motorcycles accelerate more rapidly than any other machines on two wheels. They reach such extreme speeds that they need parachutes to slow them down at the end of the race.

❯ DIFFERENT CLASSES

Drag riders compete in different classes of race. Classes for road-legal motorcycles allow amateurs to compete, while other classes involve custom-built machines run by pro teams. The fastest class is known as Top Fuel, in which just about anything goes. The Funny Motorcycles category features souped-up road-legal motorcycles. In the Pro Stock category, the motorcycles must meet a strict set of restrictions, placing the emphasis on rider skill.

TIMES OVER 0.24 MILE (400 M)

Road-legal motorcycles
9–10 seconds

Pro Stock
7.5–8 seconds

Funny Motorcycles
6.5–7 seconds

SPEED RECORD

U.S. rider Larry "Spiderman" McBride (born 1958) has been racing drag motorcycles for more than 40 years. He has broken the world record several times, and set his fastest time in 2019 at age 61 at Rockingham Dragway in North Carolina. He covered the 0.24 miles (400 m) in just 5.607 seconds, reaching a top speed of 262 miles (423 km) per hour. McBride is famed for riding his motorcycle lying on his belly to improve aerodynamics and maximize speed.

The long wheelie bar at the back stops the motorcycle from rearing up as it accelerates.

Top fuel
6 seconds

TOP FUEL

The custom-built motorcycles in the Top Fuel category have huge engines that generate up to 1,500 hp of power. That's 10 times the power of a large road motorcycle. The motorcycles accelerate from 0 to 99 miles (160 km) per hour in just over one second. They use a special fuel made from nitromethane (also called "nitr'"). Nitro is an explosive mixture that burns much more quickly than gas, and nitro engines produce more than twice the power of gas engines. During a race, the engines burn three liters of fuel per second.

BATTLE

In the early 2000s, two extreme streamliner motorcycles (see page 7) battled for the title of fastest vehicle on two wheels, trading records at the Bonneville Salt Flats in Utah. These long, bullet-shaped vehicles look more like rockets than motorcycles, and their riders are known as pilots.

ACK ATTACK

Top 1 Oil-Ack Attack first broke the record in 2006, and regained it in 2010, becoming the first motorcycle to exceed 372.8 miles (600 km) per hour. It was piloted each time by American rider Rocky Robinson (born 1961). Ack Attack was designed and built by American Mike Akatiff (born 1945, right). Akatiff's team plans to attempt to break the 400 miles (644 km) per hour barrier in future rides at Salar de Uyuni salt flats in Bolivia.

WWW.TOPOIL.COM

Ack Attack is powered by twin engines, one in front of the other. The pilot lies on their back feet-first to make it as aerodynamic as possible.

TRADING RECORDS

September 5, 2006
BUB Seven | 351 miles
(565 km) per hour

September 3, 2006
Top 1 Oil-Ack Attack | 343 miles
(552 km) per hour

BUB SEVEN

The BUB Seven took the record from Ack Attack twice, first in 2006 and again in 2009. Each time, it was piloted by American rider Chris Carr (born 1967). The motorcycle's designer, Denis Manning (born 1946), was inspired by the aerodynamic shape of a salmon.

FASTEST WOMAN ON TWO WHEELS

In 2018, American Valerie Thompson (born 1967) piloted the BUB Seven to a speed of 328.7 miles (529 km) per hour, making her the fastest female motorcycle racer. Thompson plans a future attempt on the overall record, and hopes to become the fastest racer ever, male or female.

September 24, 2009
BUB Seven | 367 miles (591 km) per hour

September 26, 2008
Top 1 Oil-Ack Attack | 361 miles (581 km) per hour

September 25, 2010
Top 1 Oil-Ack Attack | 376.5 miles (606 km) per hour

EXTREME
MACHINES

These custom motorcycles are among the biggest, most extreme vehicles on two wheels. They have huge engines and pack an extreme punch of power. It takes a brave rider to take these monsters out to their maximum speed.

TOMAHAWK

The Tomahawk was a **concept motorcycle** built by Dodge in 2003. It was powered by a huge 8.3-liter engine, designed originally for the Dodge Viper sports car. The Tomahawk was not road-legal and only nine were ever built. Dodge claimed that it could reach a top speed of more than 372.8 miles (600 km) per hour. However, nobody has ever dared to take it over 99 miles (160 km) per hour!

LM 847

Like the Tomahawk, this huge motorcycle, from French manufacturer Lazareth, has four wheels, with two side-by-side at the front and rear. Each wheel has its own separate **suspension**, which allows the rider to lean into turns as they would on a two-wheeled motorcycle. The LM 847 is fully road-legal, and has been manufactured in a limited edition of just 10 motorcycles.

WRAITH

U.S. manufacturer Confederate Motorcycles specializes in limited-edition custom motorcycles. Made to order, the Wraith has a 2.2-liter engine, which gives out a fearsome rumble. The body is carved entirely from blocks of solid aluminium, making the motorcycle strong but lightweight. It has a top speed of 161.5 miles (260 km) per hour.

GLOSSARY

aerodynamics
The study of the way a solid object moves through a liquid or gas. Vehicles are given aerodynamic shapes that allow air to flow smoothly around them when they move at high speeds.

altitude
A measure of the height of an object or a location above sea level.

concept motorcycle
A motorcycle that manufacturers make to test out a new idea.

cylinder
A chamber inside an engine where fuel burns to drive a piston up and down. The piston produces the power to turn the wheels.

drag
A force that slows an object down when it moves through the air.

exhaust
The waste gases produced by the engine as it burns its fuel.

fairing
A smooth metal or plastic covering that is added to a vehicle to allow it to cut through the air more easily.

forks
Rods that connect the front wheel of a motorcycle to its frame.

gas engine
An engine that is powered by burning the liquid oil-based fuel gas.

grip
The friction generated between a tire and the surface of the road, which stops a wheel from skidding sideways when taking turns.

high-performance
Description of a motorcycle built to be ridden at high speeds.

production motorcycle
A motorcycle that is made in large quantities in a factory to be sold to the public.

stages
Separate races held each day during a long endurance event or a rally.

supercharger
A device fitted to an engine to increase its power. The supercharger forces air into the cylinders to make the fuel burn more quickly. An engine fitted with a supercharger is called a "supercharged engine."

suspension
A system of springs and shock absorbers that connects the wheels of a motorcycle to its frame.

transmission
The part of a motorcycle that transfers the power of the engine to the wheels via a gearbox.

valve
A device fitted to a pipe that allows air or liquid to flow in just one direction.

SPEED FILE

FASTEST STREAMLINER MOTORCYCLE
Ack Attack
Max speed 410 miles (**606 km**) per hour
Set 2010

FASTEST WOMAN ON A MOTORCYCLE
Valerie Thompson / BUB 7 Streamliner
Max speed 328 miles (**529 km**) per hour
Set 2018

FASTEST DRAG MOTORCYCLE
Larry McBride
Max speed 262 miles (**423 km**) per hour
Set 2019

FASTEST PRODUCTION MOTORCYCLE
Kawasaki Ninja H2R
Max speed 248 miles (**400 km**) per hour
Set 2016

FASTEST MOTOGP MOTORCYCLE IN A RACE
Andrea Dovizioso / Ducati
Max speed 221 miles (**356 km**) per hour
Set 2018

FASTEST ELECTRIC PRODUCTION MOTORCYCLE
Lightning LS-218
Max speed 218 miles (**351 km**) per hour
Set 2014

FASTEST WHEELIE
Ted Brady
Max speed 218 miles (**351 km**) per hour
Set 2017

FASTEST SPEED ON A QUAD MOTORCYCLE
Terry Wilmeth / Yamaha 700 Raptor
Max speed 196 miles (**316 km**) per hour
Set 2008

FASTEST SPEED ON A 'WALL OF DEATH'
Guy Martin
Max speed 78 miles (**126 km**) per hour
Set 2016

INDEX